The 2020 Guide For Utah Housing Grants And Assistance

Timothy L Carver & Clint T Carver

Table of Contents

Introduction

"We Got the Grant!"

"No one is going to give us free money, Dad."

That was my son's response when I first told him and his wife about grants for first-time home buyers.

My son Clint, his wife and 3 year old daughter were living in an apartment and trying to save enough money to get into a home.

Clint was working and going to school so saving for a down payment was pretty challenging.

"This is a real program," I said. "It's sponsored by the government. And I'm pretty sure you can qualify."

"I still don't believe it," he said. "No one is going to give you free money without some catch to it."

"Why don't you call this number and find out?" I said.

He did. Guess what?

They got the $5,000 grant! It was enough to get him and his young family into their first home!

The <u>sad news</u> is that many people are like Clint was. They are unaware that these grants are available.

The News Gets Worse!

According to the U.S. Census, Utah is the third fastest-growing state in the nation, with a 1.9 percent growth in population from 2017 to 2018.

KSL.com recently published an article illustrating the percent of increase in the cost of homes in Utah since 1991. It's an astounding **276%!!!**

And it doesn't look like things are going to slow down any time soon.

Jim Wood, Ivory-Boyer Senior Fellow at the Gardner Policy Institute, stated, "Housing prices in Utah will continue to increase at rates well above the national average due to relatively high rates of population and economic growth."

And guess who's getting hurt the most?

Yep, it's the first-time homebuyer.

But There's GOOD NEWS!

There are federal, state and local helps available for the first-time home buyer. These helps come in the form of grants, special loan programs and down payment assistance.

Unfortunately **VERY FEW** people are aware of the programs!

So we decided to team up and create a SIMPLE and QUICK guide for tracking down these programs.

With <u>more than a decade</u> of combined experience in the real estate <u>and</u> mortgage worlds, we've found that we especially enjoy helping first-time home buyers!

So here's what you'll find in this guide:

- **Details** about federal, state and local agencies that provide financial housing assistance for specific cities and counties in Utah
- **Qualification requirements** for each program
- **Contact information** so you can call and speak directly to personnel

It's easy! It's quick! And it's VERY valuable! It can save **THOUSANDS OF DOLLARS** on the purchase of a home.

So c'mon inside! We've got some great information for you!

You could be one of those saying, **"We got the grant!"**

Tim Carver
Clint Carver

Want Free Help?

Would you like some free help in finding if there is a housing grant, down payment assistance or a low-interest loan in your area?

We offer FREE assistance to home buyers <u>anywhere</u> in Utah.

We can help you:

- Locate any grants or assistance in your city, nearby city or county.
- Determine if you qualify.
- Apply for the assistance.
- Locate a lender that works with these programs.
- Find a great home that fits in your budget.
- Negotiate a fair price.
- Complete the contract paperwork.
- Help you set up the inspection and title work.

As your real estate agent we can perform all of the services at NO COST to you.

Sound too good to be true?

It's not.

Real estate agents receive their commission from the seller of the home, not the buyer. So you can hire an outstanding real estate agent and receive all of the services for <u>free</u>. The agent will be paid by the seller.

If you live in any of the areas we serve (Box Elder, Davis, Salt Lake and Weber counties) we'll be happy to serve as your real estate agent at no cost to you.

If you live in other counties in Utah we are happy to connect you with outstanding real estate agents in your area who will provide the same free services.

Check out our **ABOUT US** page for contact information.

Best wishes in getting financial assistance and a home of your own!

Tim Carver
Clint Carver

Nationwide Housing Assistance Programs

The Chenoa Fund

The **Chenoa Fund** is an affordable housing program provided by CBC Mortgage Agency (CBCMA), a federally chartered governmental entity. CBCMA has a mission to increase affordable and sustainable homeownership, specifically for creditworthy, low- and moderate-income individuals.

CBCMA provides the down payment to assist a buyer with a home purchase. There are no first-time borrower requirements.

Website

https://chenoafund.org/homebuyer/providing-down-payment-assistance-on-fha-and-conventional-loans/

The following are the primary programs offered by CBCMA:

FHA Loans

There are three options offered for down payment assistance with FHA-insured mortgages:

- *Chenoa Fund Edge Program.* The borrower receives a 30-year term, 0% rate, no payment, second mortgage. Borrowers need to meet the minimum FICO score of 620 and have a qualifying income less than or equal to 115% of the median income for the county in which the borrower will live. The loan is forgiven as soon as the borrower makes 36 consecutive on-time payments on the FHA first mortgage.

- *Chenoa Fund Repayable Second Program.* With this program, the borrower does not have any income restrictions. There are two options for the repayable second. The borrower can choose a 10-year repayable second at 0% interest rate or a 30-year repayable second at 5% interest rate. Borrowers will need to meet the minimum FICO score of 620. This assistance must be repaid in full.

- *Chenoa Fund Rate Advantage Program.* With this program, the borrower is able to lock their first mortgage at a market comparable rate. Borrowers will need to meet the minimum FICO score requirement of 640, have a debt to income ratio of 50% or less, and have qualifying income less than or equal to 115% of the median income for the county in which the borrower will live.

Conventional Loans

CBCMA offers down payment assistance to those who qualify for a 97% LTV conventional first mortgage under Fannie Mae's HomeReady® program for low to moderate income borrowers, with expanded eligibility for homes in low-income communities. If a buyer does not fit the HomeReady® criteria but may not have the resources for a larger down payment on a home purchase, the buyer may still qualify for the standard conventional 97% loan-to-value program and receive assistance from CBC Mortgage Agency for the down payment and some closing costs.

There are no household income limits under a conventional standard 97% LTV program. A buyer will need to meet minimum credit score of 640 and all other guidelines for the conventional standard 97% LTV or HomeReady® programs.

For Which Cities and Counties in Utah Does This Apply?

There are no geographic restrictions. This assistance is available nationwide.

Where Can I Learn More?

For more information about this program:
Call 866-563-3507
Email: *info@chenoafund.org*

> **NOTE**: HomeReady® *is a registered trademark of Fannie Mae.*

The Dream Maker

The Dream Maker program offers a grant to low-to-moderate income service members, veterans, reservists and the National Guard who are purchasing their first home. The grant is provided by the PenFed Foundation, a national non-profit organization focused on financially assisting those who serve in the military.

The amount of the grant is determined by a 2-to-1 match of the borrower's contribution to their mortgage. For example, if a borrower saves $1,500 toward down payment and/or closing costs, PenFed will match that amount with a grant of $3,000. The maximum grant given by PenFed is $5,000. Grant approvals are contingent upon available funding.

Website

https://penfedfoundation.org/

Who Is Eligible?

In order to be eligible buyers must:

- Be active duty, reserve, National Guard or veteran.
- Not have owned a home for last 3 years or lost a home through divorce or disaster.
- Meet the income guidelines (see website).

What Are the Requirements?

Requirements include:

- Participants must be pre-qualified through a private lender of their choice.
- Home must be a single family dwelling (includes townhomes and condos).
- All types of mortgages are accepted (VA, FHA, conventional).
- All loans must be 97% loan-to-value or less.
- All loans must have a 30-year re-payment term and a fixed rate.

How Do I Learn More?

Contact information:

https://penfedfoundation.org/about-us/contact-us/

SDA Single Family Direct Loan

The **USDA Single Family Direct Loan** is offered by the United States Department of Agriculture (USDA). It helps low and very low-income applicants obtain housing in eligible rural areas by providing a loan directly from the USDA. The interest rate can be as low as 1%.

Payment assistance is a type of subsidy that reduces the mortgage payment for a short time. The amount of assistance is determined by the adjusted family income.

There are important differences between the "guaranteed" and the "direct" programs. Borrowers with incomes up to 115% of U.S. median income can qualify for guaranteed loans. Direct borrowers have incomes of not more than 80% of area median.

Website

https://www.rd.usda.gov/programs-services/single-family-housing-direct-home-loans/ut

Who Can Apply for This Program?

Applicants must:

- Be without decent, safe and sanitary housing.
- Be unable to obtain a loan from other resources on terms and conditions that they can reasonably be expected to meet.
- Agree to occupy the property as the primary residence.
- Have the legal capacity to incur a loan obligation.
- Meet citizenship or eligible noncitizen requirements.
- Not be suspended or debarred from participation in federal programs.
- Repay all or a portion of the subsidy received when the title to the property transfers or the borrower is no longer living in the dwelling.

How Can the Funds Be Used?

Loan funds may be used to help low-income individuals/families purchase homes in rural areas. Funds can be used to build, repair, renovate or relocate a home, or to purchase and prepare sites, including providing water and sewage.

What Are the Eligibility Requirements?

See website.

How Much Can I Borrow?

The maximum loan amount an applicant may qualify for will depend on the applicant's repayment ability. The applicant's ability to repay a loan considers such factors as income, debt and assets.

How Can I Learn More?

Contact Lori Silva, Housing Programs Director, at 801-524-4323.

USDA Single Family Guaranteed Loan

USDA Single Family Guaranteed Loan is a loan that is backed by the United States Department of Agriculture (USDA) for eligible rural and suburban home buyers. It provides 100% financing (no down payment required) with reduced mortgage insurance premiums and offers below-market mortgage rates.

In this program the USDA does <u>not</u> issue the loan but guarantees the loan offered through participating local lenders. This guarantee allows lenders to offer a lower interest rate, even without a down payment. If buyers put little or no money down they will have to pay a mortgage insurance premium.

There are important differences between the "guaranteed" and the "direct" programs. Borrowers with incomes up to 115% of U.S. median income can qualify for guaranteed loans, while direct borrowers must have incomes of not more than 80% of area median.

Website

https://www.rd.usda.gov/programs-services/single-family-housing-guaranteed-loan-program/ut

What Are the Income Limits?

Income limits vary by location and depend on the size of the household. To locate the loan guarantee income limit for the county/city where you live, refer to this map:

https://eligibility.sc.egov.usda.gov/eligibility/welcome Action.do?pageAction=sfp

Who Is Eligible for This Program?

Applicants must:

- Meet income-eligibility
- Agree to personally occupy the dwelling as their primary residence.
- Be a US citizen, US non-citizen national or qualified alien.
- Have the legal capacity to incur the loan obligation.
- Have not been suspended from participation in federal programs.
- Demonstrate the willingness to meet credit obligations in a timely manner.
- Purchase a property that meets all program criteria.

How May Funds Be Used?

Funds backed by loan guarantees may be used for:

- New or existing residential property to be used as a permanent residence.
- Closing costs and reasonable/customary expenses associated with the purchase.
- A site with a new or existing dwelling.

- Repairs associated with the purchase of an existing dwelling.

How Can I Learn More?

Contact Lori Silva, Housing Programs Director, at 801-524-4323.

Veterans Administration Home Loan

Veterans Administration (VA) Home Loans are loans specifically designed for members of the regular military, veterans, reservists and National Guard. These loans are not provided through the Veterans Administration but through private lenders. But because the VA guarantees a portion of these loans against loss, the private lenders are able to offer more favorable terms.

What Are the Benefits of a VA Guaranteed Loan?

Benefits include:

- No down payment is required (unless required by the lender).
- No mortgage insurance is required.
- A VA loan can be assumed by qualified persons.
- VA rules limit the amount you can be charged for closing costs.
- VA requirements insure the property is safe and sound.
- The VA staff provides assistance if owner becomes delinquent on the loan.
- A lender can't charge a penalty fee when loan is paid off early.

Website

https://www.benefits.va.gov/homeloans/resources_ve teran.asp#Benefit

Who Is Eligible?

Eligible applicants include:

- Veterans who meet service length requirements.
- Service members on active duty who have served a minimum period.
- Certain reservists and National Guard members.
- Certain surviving spouses of deceased veterans.

Are There Any Other Requirements?

Additional requirements include:

- The home must be a primary residence.
- Participants must have a valid Certificate of Eligibility from the VA.
- VA has no minimum credit score requirement but most lenders do.

Veterans are encouraged to contact several lenders to determine the best loan rate and to get pre-approved. The *Consumer Financial Protection Bureau* has tools and resources to help home buyers:

https://www.consumerfinance.gov/owning-a-home/

How Can I Learn More?

VA info sheet:

https://www.benefits.va.gov/BENEFITS/factsheets/homeloans/VA_Guaranteed_Home_Loans.pdf

Utah Housing
Assistance Programs

Utah Housing Corporation

Utah Housing Corporation (UHC) was created in 1975 by Utah legislation to help provide mortgage loans at reasonable interest rates for low and moderate income persons. Utah Housing Corporation offers:

- Five different mortgage programs.
- Down payment and closing cost assistance.

Website

https://utahhousingcorp.org/

It is important to understand that UHC does <u>not</u> provide loans. Loans are provided through "Participating Lenders". For a list of Participating Lenders:

https://utahhousingcorp.org/lenders/participatingLender

> **NOTE**: *Be sure to specify to lenders that you want a Utah Housing loan.*

UHC Mortgage Programs

1. **FirstHome:** This mortgage program typically has the lowest interest rate. It is geared toward first-time homebuyers with a credit score of 660 or higher, whose income and purchase price is below the posted limits. Income limits are based on household members 18 and older.

2. **HomeAgain:** This program is for homebuyers with a credit score of 660 or higher. It also includes those who have previously owned a home or are first-time homebuyers who do not qualify for "FirstHome". This program does <u>not</u> have a purchase price limit but does have annual income limits based on qualifying income.

3. **NoMI:** Utah Housing has announced that for a limited time, a new down payment assistance grant for lower income borrowers purchasing a home with a Utah Housing NoMI loan. Borrowers eligible for a non-repayable, NoMI Grant may receive at closing:

   a. $1500 with annual income of 80% Area Median Income or below
   b. $2500 with annual income of 50% Area Median Income or below

4. **Score:** This program is for homebuyers with a credit score of 620 or higher. This program offers a loan to homebuyers who have recovered from previous credit challenges. This program has a purchase price limit and annual income limits based on qualifying income.

5. **Veterans Grant:** The Utah legislature appropriated funds to help veterans purchase a home in Utah. This grant is for members of the military or veterans who separated in the last 5 years and are a first-time Utah homebuyer. Eligible veterans could receive up to $2,500 cash when they purchase a home. This grant does <u>not</u> require repayment.

Do I Qualify?

To obtain down payment assistance from Utah Housing, a buyer must first qualify for a Utah Housing Corp mortgage loan. A Participating Lender will help determine how much down payment and closing cost assistance will be needed and help the buyer select a Utah Housing Corp home loan that fits best.

How Can I Learn More?

Email: mortgageuthc.org
Phone: 801-902-8200

Fair Credit Foundation

The Fair Credit Foundation is a non-profit entity that helps individuals/families save toward a down payment through an Individual Development Account (IDA) program.

The IDA program matches $3 for every dollar you save. You can save up to $1,500 and your savings will be matched with an additional $4,500. This money must be used toward a down payment on a first home, tuition at an accredited school (or books at a school's bookstore), small business startup/capitalization, or assistive technologies for work related activities.

Website

https://faircredit.org/services/savings-programs/

What Are The Qualifications?

To qualify for the IDA program you must:

- Be a Utah resident.
- Be at least 18 years old.
- Own less than $10,000 in net assets (excluding one house and one car).

Are There Income Limits?

Yes. See website.

Are There Additional Requirements?

Yes. IDA program participants must also:

- Complete 8 hours of financial training courses.
- Maintain regular contact with a financial counselor.
- Participate in asset-specific training.
- Make monthly deposits of at least $15 and not more than $62.50.
- Save in the program for a minimum of 12 months (but not more than 36).

Do I Qualify?

Answer this questionnaire to see if you qualify:

https://faircredit.org/eforms/ida-qualifier-quiz/7/

How Can I Learn More?

Call (800) 351-4195 or (801) 483-0999

County Housing
Assistance Programs

The BRAG Program

Box Elder, Cache and Rich Counties

The BRAG First Time Home Buyer program is sponsored by the Bear River Association of Governments (BRAG). This program provides valuable education for the first-time home buyer and funding for closing costs or down payment assistance in the form of a deferred, no-interest loan.

Funding in the form of a deferred no-interest loan to help with closing costs or down payment assistance for your first home.

Website

Currently no website available.

How Much Assistance Is Given?

The maximum assistance is the lesser of $1,600 or the total unpaid settlement costs listed on the final settlement statement.

NOTE: *Applicants who complete the First Time Home Buyer Education workshop one month or more in advance of their purchase agreement and mortgage application will be eligible for an additional $400 for a maximum loan of $2,000.*

Who is Eligible for This Program?

Anyone buying their first home in Box Elder, Cache, or Rich Counties who meets HUD income guidelines is eligible. Contact Jeff Kearl (info below) for income guidelines.

What Homes Can Be Purchased with This Program?

The home can be:

- Single family dwelling.
- A town home or condo.
- A manufactured home on permanent foundation on buyer's property.
- New construction (check with BRAG for restrictions).

Do I Have to Pay Back the Loan?

Yes. The loan is a deferred no-interest loan and will be secured by a trust deed and note. The note will be held by BRAG and is payable when the property is resold, refinanced, rented, or title is transferred.

Does it matter which mortgage lender I choose to work with?

No. BRAG will work with most mortgage lenders.

How Can I Learn More?

Jeff Kearl
Phone: 435.752.72422
Email: *jeffk@brag.utah.gov*

Community Development Corp of Utah

Salt Lake County, Salt Lake City, Taylorsville

Community Development Corporation of Utah (CDCU) is a non-profit organization that provides housing assistance for those living in Salt Lake City, Salt Lake County and Taylorsville. The focus is to help low-to-moderate income families make homeownership a reality through two programs:

- Down payment assistance
- The HomeFit Mortgage

Website for Down Payment Assistance

https://cdcutah.org/housing-services/downpayment-assistance

Website for HomeFit Mortgage

https://cdcutah.org/homefit-mortgage

Down Payment Assistance

This is a no payment, no interest loan that is forgivable after a period of time. The funds can be used to cover the down payment or closing costs. There are a limited number available each year and qualified applicants will receive their financial award on a first come, first qualified basis-no waiting list, no funds reserved.

Down payment assistance funds are NOT available in Sandy, South Jordan, West Jordan, and West Valley City. Please check directly with these municipalities for additional information.

What Are the Requirements?

- Applicants must be household income eligible at or below 80% of the Area Median Income (see website).
- Applicants must contribute 1% of the purchase price in personal funds
- Maximum debt-to-income ratio: 45%
- Applicants must be under contract (have an accepted offer to purchase a property) at the time of submitting an application.

The HomeFit Mortgage

The HomeFit™ Mortgage finances 100% of the purchase price of the home through two loans – the first 80% is covered through a conventional loan, and the remaining 20% is a second mortgage that is serviced and managed by CDCU's affiliate, Community Development Fund of Utah.

Because of the two loans, there is NO requirement for mortgage insurance. The interest rate on the second mortgage is 2% higher than the interest rate on the first. Even with the higher interest rate, the combined monthly mortgage payments of the two loans are less than they would be on a FHA loan.

What Are the Requirements for HomeFit Mortgage?

- Minimum credit score of 620 (including at least one year of credit history).
- Maximum DTI (total debt, including mortgage payments to total income) of 43%.
- Two years of employment history.
- 2% minimum contribution towards closing costs. 1% of the contribution must be the borrower's own funds. The other 1% can be gifted.
- Reserved savings (even after your 2% contribution, we like to see that you still have some savings in case of emergencies).
- Completed HUD-approved home buyer education class.

How Can I Learn More?

Contact CDCU:
501 East 1700 South Salt Lake City, Utah 84105
Email: *info@CDCutah.org*
Phone: 801-994-7222

Davis County Down Payment Assistance

The Davis County Down Payment Assistance program is a grant of up to $10,000 to assist first-time home buyers in Davis County. All cities within Davis County are eligible except Fruit Heights, South Weber, Layton, or Clearfield City. Layton and Clearfield have their own housing assistance programs (see Table of Contents).

The grant can be used to:

- Pay up to 50% of the down payment required by the mortgagee for the purchase.
- Pay any or all of the reasonable closing costs associated with the home purchase.
- Pay all or part of the premium for mortgage insurance required up-front. This would include the cost for private mortgage insurance.
- Pay for principal write-downs on the home loan.

Website

http://www.daviscommunityhousing.com/other-programs

What Kind of Homes Can Be Purchased?

Eligible properties must be zoned for residential use only and are limited to single family residences such as: condominiums, town homes, and combination of manufactured housing and lot. Duplexes and new construction, including never occupied homes, are not eligible.

What Are the Eligibility Requirements?

Applicants (includes all household members over 18 even if they will not be considered a buyer) must meet one of the definitions of a first time home buyer described as:

- An individual who has not owned a home, except a mobile home not affixed to a permanent foundation, during the 3-year period prior to the purchase of a home with this assistance.
- A single parent who has only owned a home with a former spouse while married.
- A displaced homemaker and has only owned a home with a spouse.

Are There Income Limits?

Yes. Check the website.

Are There Additional Requirements?

Yes. Applicants must:

- Be a U.S. Citizen or Permanent Resident Alien and be 18 years or older.
- Complete a HUD approved homebuyer education course and provide a homebuyer certificate of course completion. Certificate should be provided within one week of application for the buyer's benefit.
- Complete and submit all required forms and verifications to the Davis Community Housing Authority (DCHA) as per the application instructions.

Is There a Limit on the Price of the Home?

Yes. Homes cannot exceed $325,000.

Am I Required to Repay the Grant?

Any funds received through this program will be forgiven at a declining rate over a 5-year time period from the date of closing. If buyers sell, exchange, transfer title, obtain a second mortgage, or decide to refinance for any reason within the first 5 years from the date of purchase, a pro-rata share of the funds provided by the DCHA must be repaid by the home buyers.

How Do I Apply?

http://www.daviscommunityhousing.com/other-programs

How Can I Learn More?

Contact Mary Swanstrom at 801-939-9198 for questions and for a qualification review prior to submitting an offer on a home.

Self-Help Homes

Utah, Wasatch and Washington Counties

Self-Help Homes is a housing program for individuals and families living in in specific cities in Summit, Utah, Wasatch and Washington counties. This program helps low income participants achieve homeownership through sweat equity. Sweat equity is the labor home buyers put into building their home.

Self-Help Homes uses the Mutual Self-Help Housing model to assist in constructing homes of five to twelve individual and families in a group. Everyone in the group helps construct the homes under the general supervision of a Self-Help Homes construction superintendent. No one moves into their home until all of the homes in the group are complete.

All of the homes are single-family homes, usually with an unfinished basement or a second story living space with a two-car garage. Lot sizes vary depending on the community where they are located. All homes average approximately 1,350 square feet on the main level.

Website

http://www.selfhelphomes.org/

What Are the Requirements?

- Income must be at or below 80% of the area median income on the table below AND you must earn a minimum income of around $35,000.00/per year in Washington County, $37,000.00/per year in Utah County and $39,000.00/per year in Wasatch County.

- Credit score of 640 or higher and at least two open lines of credit for a consecutive 12 month period (within in the last 24 months). You cannot have any collections or judgements within the last six months, or more than one 30-day late payment within the last year.

- Must be willing to work at least 35 hours per week on all the houses within your group until they are finished (an average of 8-10 months). Each family must work on Saturdays from 8:00 a.m. to 2:00 p.m.
- For additional requirements see website.

How Can I Learn More?

http://www.selfhelphomes.org/contact-self-help-homes-contact

Tooele County CROWN Program

The Tooele County CROWN (Credit-to-OWN) program was created by Utah Housing Corporation (UHC) in 1993 to provide homeownership opportunities for low-income families in Tooele County.

CROWN addresses the needs of people who face the challenge of rent being too high, homes being unavailable, and/or poor redit that prevents them from purchasing a home.

CROWN is a 15 year rent-to-own program. The home is available for purchase by the household living in it when the home reaches the end of a 15 year compliance period. The home is available for purchase at a discounted price.

Website

http://www.co.tooele.ut.us/housing/renttoown.html

What is the Current Rental Cost?

The rent is $819 to $830 for a 4 bed/2 bath home.

Are Utilities Included with the Rent?

No. Tenants are responsible for paying their own utilities. In addition:

- Tenants are responsible for typical homeowner maintenance (e.g. mowing lawn, changing furnace filters, etc.).

Does Rent Increase?

The CROWN program is funded with Low Income Housing Tax Credits (LIHTC) funds. The rents are subject to these rent limitations and do not typically increase as often or as much as a market rent can.

What is Included with the Home?

All homes have:

- A two-car garage
- Central air

Are There Income Limits and Additional Requirements?

Yes, see the info on the website.

How Can I Learn More?

Contact Tooele County Housing Authority Main Office
at:
66 W. Vine Street
Tooele, UT 84074
Phone: 435-882-7875

Utah County Loan-to-Own

Utah County Loan-to-Own program is designed to help people struggling to come up with a down payment or closing costs. This is a 0% interest loan of up to $10,000 that can be used for down payment and/or closing costs.

This is offered through the Provo City Redevelopment Agency for income-qualified buyers who have not owned a home within the last three years. No portion of the loan is forgivable.

Purchase price of the home may not exceed HUD limit. Currently $337,250 for both existing and new homes as of August 15, 2019.

Website

https://www.provo.org/departments/redevelopment/ services/loan-to-own-program

Which Cities in Utah County Are Eligible?

As of July 1, 2017, all cities are eligible except Eagle Mountain, Woodland Hills, Highland, Fairfield and Provo (Provo has their own program, see Provo in Table of Contents).

This is an interested 0% interest, deferred loan. No payment is due as long as the applicant(s) continue to own and live in the home as their primary residence.

Balance is due upon sale or when property ceases to be owner occupied. You must be able to put down $1,000 of your own money. $5,000 penalty if sold or vacated within two years of closing.

How Much Can I Qualify For?

Determined by a HUD formula and your credit score, you may qualify for up to $25,000. See website for details.

What Are the Requirements?

- You must be qualified with a bank or other financial institution for the first mortgage.
- The total income of all family members over 18 must be less than the Income Limits (see website).
- Must be on current job a minimum of six months.
- Must not have owned a home in the last three years.
- Must have a mid-credit score above 650 with no unsatisfied judgments or collections.
- Both spouses are required to be on our loan (regardless of whether they are on the first) and must meet the credit requirement.
- Liquid assets cannot exceed $15,000 at time of closing.
- All household members over 18 must pass a background check.

How Can I Learn More?

For further questions, call 801-852-6160.

Weber County Housing Assistance

Weber Housing Authority Homeownership Assistance is currently not available.

How Can I Learn More?

For more information, contact:
Weber Housing Authority
Office Hours: Monday, Wednesday, and Friday 9:00 AM to 5:00 PM
Phone: 801-399-8691
Email: *awatkins@co.weber.ut.us*

City Housing
Assistance Programs

Clearfield City's Down Payment Assistance

Clearfield City's Down Payment Assistance is currently unavailable.

However, funds do become available from time to time. Contact Mary Swanstrom below for updates.

How Can I Learn More?

For additional information contact:
Mary Swanstrom at 801-939-9198.

At Home In Layton

At Home in Layton is a program offered through the Layton City Community Development Block Grant Program to low and moderate income individuals and families.

The assistance is offered as a grant that can be used for up to 50% of the required down payment, closing costs or principal reduction. The grant will be offered in $7,500 increments. Grant money will be provided to buyer's title company at the time of closing.

Website

https://www.laytoncity.org/LC/CD/EconomicDevelop ment

What Are the Requirements?

- Qualifying buyers must meet household income levels (see website).
- Pre-approval letter from a lender
- 2018 Income Tax Returns from all household members
- Pay stubs from all working household members (Submit most recent.)
- A completed Real Estate Purchase Contract (REPC) showing a qualifying offer has been accepted

Do I Need to Repay the Grant?

If the house is sold before the end of the fifth year from the closing date, all or a portion of the grant will need to be repaid to Layton City.

How Can I Learn More?

Phone: 801-336-3770
Email: *mcloward@laytoncity.org*

Applications are accepted on a first-come first-served basis until all funds have been granted.

Own in Logan

The **Own in Logan** program provides down payment/closing cost assistance of up to $7,500 for first-time home buyers in the city limits of Logan, Utah.

Those who meet all eligibility criteria can receive a $5,000 base grant for down payment and/or closing cost assistance. They must make at least a $500 down payment of your own funds – no gifts – to qualify. The subsidy is a soft second lien and must be paid back if you sell, obtain a second mortgage, refinance, or meet other conditions.

Participants can also receive a matching grant of up to $2,500 for any additional down payment funds needed. The matched grant portion is fully forgiven if buyers occupy the home for a 10-year period.

Website

https://neighborhoodhousing.net/become-a-homeowner/buy-home-logan/

What Are the Requirements?

Requirements include:

- Applicants must qualify for a home loan (FHA, Utah Housing Corporation programs or similar insured mortgages) from a lender of their choice.
- Have not owned a home in the past three years, who currently own a trailer that is not on a permanent foundation. It can also include those who own or lease a condominium, and/or are a displaced spouse.
- Must have an annual combined household income equal to or less than 80% of the HUD median income guidelines for Cache County, based on household size (see website). Income from anyone in the household 18 or older is included.
- Housing debt, or front-end ratio, must not exceed 38%.
- Total debt-to-income ratio cannot exceed 41% (exceptions may apply – see full program policies for details).
- Applicants will be required to receive a certificate verifying participation in a HUD-approved First-time Homebuyer class or workshop (offered both online and in-person).

Do I Need to Repay the Grant?

The subsidy is a soft second lien and must be paid back if owners sell, obtain a second mortgage, refinance, or meet other conditions.

How Can I Learn More?

Contact *Neighborhood Housing Solutions* at:
195 West Golf Course Road
Logan, UT 84321
Phone: 435-753-1112

Logan Area
Owner-Builder Program

The Owner-Builder Program, also known as the Mutual Self-Help Housing Program, is a housing program that uses sweat equity to reduce the overall cost of building a home in the Logan area.

The goal of the program is to provide families with modest single-family homes with affordable monthly house payments. Through the present time, over 400 families have built their own homes in the Logan Owner-Builder Program.

Website

https://neighborhoodhousing.net/become-a-homeowner/build-your-own-home/

What Are the Eligibility Requirements?

For eligibility requirements, contact the Neighborhood Housing Solutions at 435-753-1112.

Where Are the Homes Located?

Applications are currently being accepted for subdivisions in Smithfield and Hyrum.

Do I Build the Home Alone?

No. About 5 to 8 eligible households work together to build each other's homes. All participants start and finish together. No one moves in until everyone's home is completed.

Do I Build the Entire Home?

No. There are certain things that will be subcontracted out (plumbing, electricity, etc.), but participants take part in the construction of 65% of the home.

What Kind of Homes Are Available?

Visit the website to see all floor plans.

How Can I Learn More?

Contact *Neighborhood Housing Solutions* at:
195 West Golf Course Road
Logan, UT 84321
Phone: 435-753-1112

Home Sweet Ogden

Home Sweet Ogden is a program sponsored by Ogden Utah Community Development for low-income individuals and families. This program offers homes that have been remodeled and are being sold by Ogden City.

Website

https://www.ogdencity.com/258/Home-Sweet-Ogden-Program

What Are the Requirements?

- Buyers must be owner-occupants and cannot exceed 80% of the area-wide median income.
- The seller is Ogden City.
- Earnest money must be at least $500.
- The sales price is not negotiable.
- The city will provide a home warranty from First American.
- All homes are purchased as-is and the seller will NOT contribute any monies toward the buyers' closing costs in addition to the **Own in Ogden** funds.
- Buyers MUST apply for **Own in Ogden** funds (up to $5000). Separate application required.
- See the website for additional requirements.

What Are the Income Limits?

See the website.

How Can I Learn More?

Bill Krill: *williamkrill@ogdencity.com*
Phone: 801-629-8945
Website: OgdenCityHomes.com

Shanna Dayton: *shannadayton@ogdencity.com*
Phone: 801-629-8900
Website: OgdenCityHomes.com

Own In Ogden Program

**OWN IN OGDEN FUNDS ARE CURRENTLY UNAVAILABLE UNTIL SOMETIME IN JANUARY, 2020
(Check website or contact Ogden City for updates)

Own in Ogden is an Ogden City program designed to increase home ownership in Ogden. Persons purchasing their primary residence in Ogden can receive up to a $5,000 zero interest, deferred- payment loan that is applied at closing toward down payment and closing costs.

Income-qualified, sworn Ogden City police officers and Ogden City fire fighters can receive up to a $10,000 loan when buying their primary residence in Ogden.

Up to $10,000 loans are also available to full-time, state-certified K-12 classroom teachers or administrators in schools which serve Ogden City students.

Income-qualified Ogden City employees and new hires who reside outside Ogden City boundaries, or who rent within Ogden City, can receive up to a $10,000 loan to buy a home as their primary residence in Ogden.

Website

https://www.ogdencity.com/259/Own-in-Ogden

What Are the Requirements?

- Borrower(s) must provide at least $500.00 of his/her own money toward the purchase. This is usually in the form of earnest money. This $500.00 contribution is to be verified prior to closing and allocation of funds, and cannot be included in the mortgage loan or refunded to buyer at closing.
- Buyer must also contribute any amounts needed to close the transaction in excess of the **Own in Ogden** assistance.
- See website for additional requirements.

Is the Loan Forgivable?

No. An **Own in Ogden** loan becomes due and payable in full when a borrower discontinues principal residency at the property, sells or transfers interest in the property, or defaults on any of the loan terms of the Own in Ogden.

Multi-unit dwellings are allowed only if the buyer resides in one of the units as the primary residence, and existing tenants are not displaced.

How Can I Learn More?

For more information, call or write Ogden City at:
2549 Washington Blvd., Suite 120
Ogden, UT 84401-1333
Phone: 801-629-8940

Provo Home Purchase Plus

Home Purchase Plus is a down payment assistance program for low-income first-time home buyers who wish to live in Provo City. This program is offered through the Provo City Redevelopment Agency.

Buyers must qualify for a first mortgage through a lender of their choice. The down payment assistance comes in the form of a 0% interest, deferred payment loan up to $10,000 (as based on need and determined by HUD formula). No payment is due on the loan as long as the applicant continues to own and live in the home as their primary residence.

> **NOTE**: A first-time home buyer is defined as someone who has had no ownership of a principal residence during the 3-year period ending on the date of the purchase of the property. This includes a spouse or partner. If either meets the above test, they are considered first-time home buyers.

Website

https://www.provo.org/departments/redevelopment/services/loan-to-own-program

What Are the Requirements?

Requirements include:

- Buyers must qualify for a first mortgage through a lender of the buyer's choice.
- The total income of all family members over 18 must be less than the Income Limits (effective July 1, 2019). Income is calculated based on the last three month's pay stubs using the actual hours worked and projecting for a year.
- Must be on current job a minimum of six months.
- Must not have owned a home in the last three years.
- Must have a mid-credit score above 650 with no unsatisfied judgments or collections.
- Liquid assets cannot exceed $15,000 at time of closing.
- All household members over 18 must pass a background check.
- Applicants must take "Pre-Home-Ownership Counseling" offered through Community Action or NeighborWorks Provo.
- Purchase price of the home may not exceed HUD limitations (currently $337,250 for existing homes and new homes - effective August 15, 2019).

How Do I Apply?

Contact the Provo City Redevelopment Agency at 801-852-6160.

West Jordan Down Payment Assistance

West Jordan Down Payment Assistance is a program offered for families from low- and moderate-income persons wishing to purchase a home in the City of West Jordan. The program provides loans for half of the required down payment and one-time closing costs for a combined total of $7,500.

Website

https://www.westjordan.utah.gov/affordablehousing

What Are the Eligibility Requirements?

- All applicants must meet income guidelines, debt ratio requirements, and cannot have owned a home within the last 24 months (see website).
- The applicant is required to provide minimum $2,000 cash out-of-pocket into the home purchase. The funds must be documented by the owner and cannot be gifted, provided by the seller, realtor, etc.
- Income for all household members over the age of 16 will be considered in the income calculation. The applicant or anyone in the household cannot have been an owner or co-owner of another home or

property within the previous 24-month period. No exceptions. Cosigners are not allowed.
- The applicant is required to provide minimum $2,000 cash out-of-pocket into the home purchase.
- See website for addition requirements.

Do I Need to Repay the Loan?

After the initial 5-year period, the loan is forgiven and no repayment is due.

How Can I Learn More?

Contact Charles Tarver at:
8000 S. Redwood Road
West Jordan, UT 84088
Phone: 801-569-5062

West Valley City Down Payment Assistance

West Valley City offers a $7,500 grant to qualified low-to-moderate income first-time home buyers. Grants are on a first come, first served basis while funds are available to those wishing to live in West Valley City.

Website

https://www.wvc-ut.gov/1366/Grant-Programs

What Are the Requirements?

Requirements include:

- All applicants must meet income guidelines (total income cannot exceed 80% AMI for household size), debt ratio requirements, and be a qualified first-time home buyer in accordance with Code of Federal Regulations (CFR). No exceptions will be made. (see website)
- Applicants must provide $2,000 cash out-of-pocket toward the purchase. The funds cannot be gifted, provided by the seller, the real estate agent, etc.

- The applicant and co-applicant must have a minimum FICO credit score rating of 550 at the time of application submission.
- West Valley City will retain a second position on the loan.
- Additional requirements can be found on the website.
- The applicant must attend and submit a completion certificate from one of the approved course providers:

  o Neighborworks: 801-539-1590
  o AAAFairCredit Foundation 1-800-351-4195
  o CDCU:801-994-7222
  o Online:www.CDCUTAH.org (Framework)

What Kind of Homes Are Eligible?

Existing single-family homes, condos and town homes that have had at least one prior owner/occupant are eligible. New construction homes are not permitted

How Can I Learn More?

West Valley City
Grants Division
4522 West 3500 South
West Valley City, UT 84120-6093
Phone: 801-963-3369

Did We Miss Something?

Are you aware of any housing assistance programs throughout the State of Utah that we missed?

If so, shoot us an email and we'll include it in our next publication.

tlcarver@comcast.net

Thanks!

About Us

Tim Carver and Clint Carver have over 15 years of combined experience in real estate, mortgages and remodeling. They currently have a best-seller book on Amazon.

The Super Simple Home Buyer's Handbook

It is a collection of our very best tips to help home buyers save money and avoid costly mistakes.

Here's what the former Director of the Utah Division of Real Estate said about the book:

"This is an excellent book. It is full of tips and pointers you may not see anyplace else. Every page is useful and helpful, and I was impressed with how much I learned from it."

Dexter Bell

Timothy L Carver

Tim Carver has been a professional educator for 37 years. He is a real estate agent with *Jody Deamer and Company* in Ogden, Utah.

He is a published author and has written a weekly real estate column in a local newspaper.

Tim has completed special training in helping clients find long-term investment properties. He also has experience in building and remodeling, along with developing and selling subdivisions.

Tim is happily married, has two children and six grandchildren. He loves to spend time with family and with golf buddies.

He can be reached at 801-458-1048 or *tlcarver@comcast.net*.

JODY DEAMER & COMPANY
a full-service real estate brokerage

Clint T Carver

Clint Carver has worked in architectural and engineering firms.

He currently works as a mortgage officer for *Beam Lending* in Layton, Utah, where he is consistently recognized as one of the top performers.

He is also a professional photographer, graphic artist and web designer.

He is happily married and has three children (and a cat and dog who are convinced they own the family home).

He can be reached at 801-784-3927 or *clintcarver3@gmail.com*.

Individual NMLS #8753442 - Company NMLS #1104582